D0934605

Animals of North America

BALD EAGLES

by Tyler Omoth

FOCUS
READERS

North Star
EDITIONS

www.northstareditions.com

Produced for North Star Editions by Red Line Editorial.

Photographs ©: Chris Hill/Shutterstock Images, cover, 1; Kandfoto/iStockphoto, 4–5; Red Line Editorial, 6; KenRinger/iStockphoto, 9; Montreal_Photos/iStockphoto, 10–11, 24 (left); Robert Palmer/Shutterstock Images, 12; Kenneth Canning/iStockphoto, 14–15, 29; Sergey Uryadnikov/Shutterstock Images, 16; Igor Kovalenko/Shutterstock Images, 19; Paul Reeves Photography/Shutterstock Images, 20–21; Lori Skelton/Shutterstock Images, 24 (top); Frank Leung/iStockphoto, 24 (right); Wildnerdpix/iStockphoto, 23, 24 (bottom); Pennsylvania Game Commission/HDOnTap and Comcast Business/AP Images, 26–27

ISBN
978-1-63517-031-3 (hardcover)
978-1-63517-087-0 (paperback)
978-1-63517-190-7 (ebook pdf)
978-1-63517-140-2 (hosted ebook)

Library of Congress Control Number: 2016951010

Printed in the United States of America
Mankato, MN
November, 2016

About the Author

Tyler Omoth is the author of more than two dozen books for children. He loves going to sporting events and taking in the sun at the beach. Omoth lives in sunny Brandon, Florida, with his wife, Mary.

TABLE OF CONTENTS

CHAPTER 1

NORTH AMERICAN BIRD

Bald eagles live mostly in the northern United States and Canada. Some also live in northern Mexico. Many eagles make their homes in Alaska.

A bald eagle soars in Alaska.

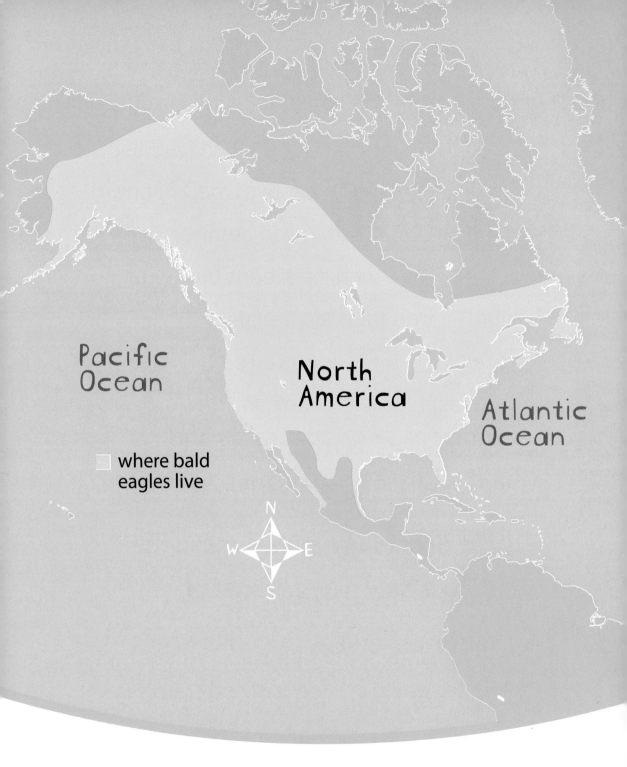

Pacific
Ocean

North
America

Atlantic
Ocean

where bald
eagles live

N
W   E
S

Bald eagles call most of North America home.

The bald eagle is a symbol of the United States. It is illegal to own a bald eagle or any part of it. Even if you find a bald eagle's feather, you cannot legally keep it.

Alaska has as many as 30,000 bald eagles. That is more than any other state.

Bald eagles spend most of their time fishing. Because of this, they stay near lakes, rivers, and other bodies of water.

In those places, fish are always available. A lake surrounded by a forest with tall trees is an ideal home for a bald eagle. The eagle can see many things from such great heights.

Male and female eagles work together to build their nest in the highest living tree they can find. An eagle's nest is large. The eagle pair builds the nest using twigs, branches, and grass.

An eagle pair sits in a nest.

CHAPTER 2

FIERCE FEATURES

The bald eagle is a **majestic** bird. Dark brown feathers cover most of a bald eagle's body. Both male and female bald eagles have white heads and tails.

Adult bald eagles are easy to spot because of their white heads.

PARTS OF A BALD EAGLE

wings

head

beak

tail

talon

They are called bald eagles because the white feathers on their heads make them look bald. A bald eagle's beak and **talons** are bright yellow. Both are very sharp.

Bald eagles are large birds. Females are bigger than males. The female wingspan can reach up to 7.5 feet (2.3 m). A male bald eagle can spread its wings up to 7 feet (2.1 m) wide. A bald eagle's size and features make it look like the fierce hunter it is.

FUN FACT

A bald eagle's feathers keep growing. When a new feather grows, it pushes out the old feather. This is called **molting**.

CHAPTER 3

THE GREAT HUNTER

Bald eagles are predatory birds. That means they hunt for their food. They use their excellent eyesight to spot fish swimming close to the water's surface. When the eagle spots its **prey**, it dives.

 Eagles can spot fish from more than 1 mile (1.6 km) away.

When diving for food, eagles can reach speeds of 100 miles per hour (161 km/h).

Bald eagles can soar up to 10,000 feet (3,048 m) in the air.

Then it grabs the fish out of the water with its sharp talons.

The biggest part of a bald eagle's diet is fish. A bald eagle will also eat small **mammals** and **waterfowl**, such as ducks. If a bald eagle spots a hawk or falcon with a meal, it uses its larger size to take the prize away.

A bald eagle has a stomach the size of a walnut. On average, a bald eagle needs only 0.5 to 1.0 pounds (0.2 to 0.5 kg) of food each day.

Sometimes, bald eagles even scavenge for food. They eat animals that are already dead. This helps them stay alive when fish or other small animals are hard to find.

An eagle snatches a fish out of the water
with its talons.

CHAPTER 4

BALD EAGLE FAMILIES

Bald eagles usually stay with the same mate their entire lives. The female eagle lays one to three eggs each year. The male and female both take turns keeping the eggs warm in the nest.

 A bald eagle sits in the nest with its chicks.

When the baby eagles hatch, they are covered in soft, gray feathers. These feathers keep the chicks warm.

After approximately three weeks, brown flight feathers start to grow. By 10 to 12 weeks, the new eagles are strong enough to leave the nest and fly on their own. A bald eagle does not get its white head and tail until it is four to five years old.

Young eagles do not yet have their white feathers.

BALD EAGLE LIFE CYCLE

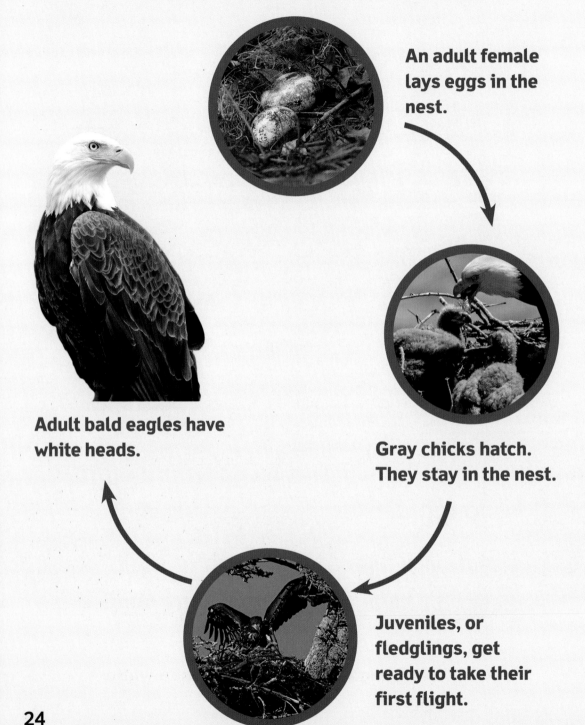

An adult female lays eggs in the nest.

Gray chicks hatch. They stay in the nest.

Juveniles, or fledglings, get ready to take their first flight.

Adult bald eagles have white heads.

Baby eagles are called eaglets or chicks. Once they are ready to fly, they are called fledglings.

When the young eagles are ready to leave the nest, they hop from the nest to a nearby branch. Then they hop back again to strengthen their wing muscles. Once they are strong enough, the eagles jump from the nest and take to the sky and soar.

EAGLE CAMS

Eagles live wild, private lives. Normally, humans cannot see into their nests. But thanks to eagle cams, viewers are able to watch eagles in their nests. Organizations across North America are placing cameras high in trees where eagles nest. These videos stream live. People can watch anytime from a computer, tablet, or smartphone. Cameras even catch eaglets taking their first flights.

Through a live eagle cam in Hanover, Pennsylvania, viewers were able to watch an eagle with its newly hatched eaglet.

FOCUS ON
BALD EAGLES

Write your answers on a separate piece of paper.

1. Write a sentence explaining the main ideas of Chapter 2.

2. Do you think owning a bald eagle or even a bald eagle's feather should be illegal? Why or why not?

3. Approximately how many bald eagles live in Alaska?
    A. 5,000
    B. 15,000
    C. 30,000

4. What might happen if an eagle didn't live by water?
    A. It might not find a mate.
    B. It might get too warm.
    C. It might have a harder time finding food.

5. What does **ideal** mean in this book?

   A. the warmest

   B. the best

   C. the worst

A lake surrounded by a forest with tall trees is an **ideal** home for a bald eagle. The eagle can see many things from such great heights.

6. What does **wingspan** mean in this book?

   A. the distance between one end of a wing and the other

   B. the length of one wing

   C. the distance an eagle can fly

The female **wingspan** can reach up to 7.5 feet (2.3 m). A male eagle can spread its wings up to 7 feet (2.1 m) wide.

Answer key on page 32.

GLOSSARY

majestic
Having great power and beauty.

mammals
Animals that give birth to live babies, have fur or hair, and produce milk.

molting
Losing older feathers, skin, or fur so new ones can grow in their place.

prey
An animal that is hunted and eaten by a different animal.

talons
Sharp claws used by birds to hunt.

waterfowl
Birds that live on or near water such as ducks or geese.

TO LEARN MORE

BOOKS

Hansen, Grace. *Bald Eagles*. Minneapolis: Abdo Kids, 2016.

Thurnherr, Paige. *Hunting with Bald Eagles*. New York: Gareth Stevens Publishing, 2012.

Waxman, Laura Hamilton. *Bald Eagles: Prey-Snatching Birds*. Minneapolis: Lerner Publications, 2016.

NOTE TO EDUCATORS

Visit **www.focusreaders.com** to find lesson plans, activities, links, and other resources related to this title.

INDEX

Answer Key: 1. Answers will vary; **2.** Answers will vary; **3.** C; **4.** C; **5.** B; **6.** A